A Child's Book
of Birds

A Child's Book of Birds

By Kathleen N. Daly

Illustrated by Fred Brenner

Doubleday & Company, Inc.   Garden City, New York

Text copyright © 1977 by Kathleen N. Daly
Illustrations copyright © 1977 by Fred Brenner
All Rights Reserved
Printed in the United States of America
9   8   7   6   5   4

Library of Congress Cataloging in Publication Data

Daly, Kathleen N.
   A child's book of birds.

   Includes index.
   SUMMARY: Brief text and pictures introduce more than twenty-
five common birds.
   1. Birds—Juvenile literature. [1. Birds]
I. Brenner, Fred. II. Title.
QL676.2.D35   598.2

ISBN 0-385-09745-X Trade
      0-385-09747-6 Prebound
Library of Congress Catalog Card Number 74-30872

The artist wishes to thank Michael Latona and Richard G. Beebe for their invaluable assistance.

Contents

A Note about Birds

BIRDS come in all shapes and sizes, from tiny
flying jewels, like the hummingbird, to huge,
proud-soaring eagles. Some of them, like sparrows
and pigeons, you may see any day in a busy street.
Others, like the wild geese, are visitors who appear
with the spring and leave in the autumn. Some
birds, like the thrushes, sing beautiful songs. Others,
like the crows, screech and yell.

All birds have two wings, and most can fly. Their
bodies are covered with feathers. Their bones are
hollow and filled with air. If you ever hold a bird
in your hand (gently!) you will find that it is very
light—almost as light as a feather.

You will also find its heart beating very fast. A
bird uses up a lot of energy to fly. It must eat and
eat all day to keep strong. So the saying, "To eat
like a bird" really means to eat a lot all day!

In this book you will find only a few birds—the
ones that you are most likely to see at first. But
there are many, many more. They all help to make
our world a beautiful place.

NOTE: Scientists have given a Latin name to every plant and animal
so that people all over the world, even though they speak many different languages, can identify them. You will find these Latin names
on pages 42–43.

Geese

ONE of the great sounds and sights of the autumn is a flock of geese flying overhead, on its way to warmer places. The geese fly in V-shaped lines, honking as they go, and when we see them we say, "Good-by until spring."

These large, handsome birds usually settle near water, but they often feed on the ground, hissing and pecking.

Sparrow

EVEN on the busiest city streets you will see sparrows. These brave little birds come quite close to people, and even feed around a horse's hoofs. Sometimes they take dust baths by the side of the road. A sparrow's twittering is a cheerful sound to hear outside your window above the noise of city traffic.

Starling

STARLINGS are common everywhere, even in the city. At first they seem like black birds, but if you look closely you will see that they are speckled with white, and that their feathers have a beautiful green and purple gloss.
Starlings are clever at copying the sounds of other birds: you may hear all kinds of twitterings and bubblings and clicks, all coming from one starling—he's like a one-man band!

Winter

Summer

Pigeons

SOME people get mad at pigeons because
they make a mess of buildings and statues and
waddle around underfoot on busy streets. But
their cooing is a friendly, gentle sound and their
feathers are beautiful shades of grays and browns.
They can fly very fast, with a clatter of wings as
they take off. Some pigeons have been trained to
carry messages attached to their legs, for great dis-
tances, and they always find their way back home
again.

Blue Jay

IF YOU see brilliant flashes of blue and hear loud screeches, repeated and answered from all around, you may be sure that there are blue jays nearby. The blue jay is a very handsome bird, one of the few really bright blue ones. He has a crest on his head. But his manners are very bad. He makes a lot of noise and tries to drive other birds away from the bird feeder. Sometimes smaller birds gang up and attack a particularly pesky blue jay.

Robin

ROBINS are often the first birds that we see in spring. We can spot them easily by their red breasts and yellow beaks. Watch them put their heads to one side, as if listening for worms. They work very hard all summer to feed their hungry, spotted babies. The American robin is named after its English cousin, "robin redbreast," which is smaller and rounder. Both kinds of robin are thrushes and they sing beautifully.

Bluebird

Wood Thrush

Thrushes

THRUSHES are well known for their beautiful songs. The notes are clear and flute-like. The nightingale, a thrush found only in Europe, is among the best of singers. So are English blackbirds. Many thrushes have spotted breasts and large eyes. They feed on worms and insects on the ground.

The BLUEBIRD is bright blue like a piece of sky, with a reddish breast. It doesn't walk about on the ground like other thrushes. Instead it drops down quickly from a perch in a nearby tree or bush.

Eagle

THE eagle is called the king of birds. He is large, and looks proud and fierce. Usually he lives in wild mountain country. Eagles feed on fish and small animals. They soar overhead on their huge

Bald Eagle

wings, watching the land and waters below. They have very sharp eyesight and can see their prey from a great distance away. For many years people hunted eagles and now there are not many left.

Golden Eagle

Hummingbirds

YOU have to be very lucky to see a hummingbird. It is the tiniest of all birds, no bigger than your little finger, and sometimes it moves so fast you can hardly see it. You might even mistake it for a large bumblebee.

It darts from flower to flower, sipping the sweet juice with its long tongue. It can fly backward, forward, up and down, or stay in one place, just like a tiny helicopter. Its wings make a humming sound, as they whir in a figure-eight pattern.

A hummingbird's eggs, laid in a nest the size of half a walnut, are no bigger than peas!

There are many kinds of hummingbirds, some with crests, ruffs, and long tails. Their feathers are as bright as jewels.

Rufous Hummingbird

Male

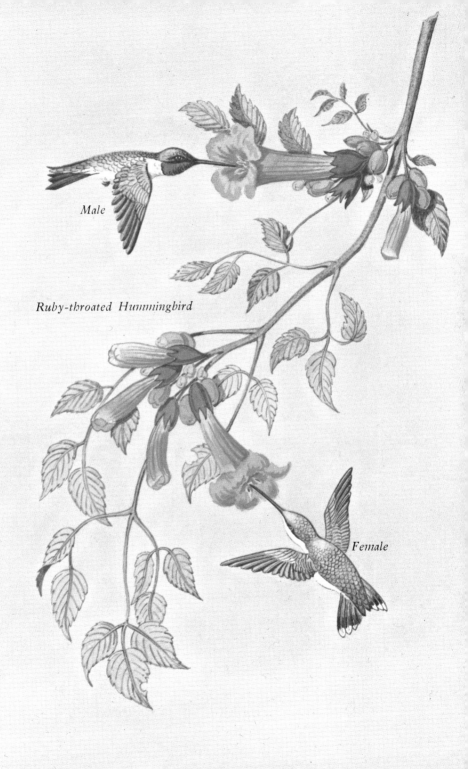

Male

Ruby-throated Hummingbird

Female

Great Horned Owl

Barn Owl

Screech Owl

Downy Woodpecker

Woodpecker

IT IS easy to spot a woodpecker. Usually you hear a drumming sound, a very quick rat-a-tat, and then you see the bird, not sitting on a branch the way most do, but climbing up the side of a tree. The woodpecker lives on the insects that he finds under the bark of an old tree. His strong toes and his tail feathers help him to hold onto the tree while he "drums."

Owls

THE members of the owl family hunt little animals such as mice. Owls hunt mostly at night. Their feathers are soft and downy, and owls can swoop down silently. Their large eyes help them to see in the dark. The owl has an eerie cry that sounds a little like *Whooo? Whooo?*

Yellowthroat

Black and White Warbler

American Redstart

Blackburnian Warbler

Yellow-rumped or Myrtle Warbler

Yellow Warbler

Warblers

To WARBLE means to sing, and that is just
what these little birds do, making our summer days
cheerful with their songs. There are many different
kinds of warblers. Lots of them are brightly
colored. Some are hard to see, for they stay in
thick bushes or among reeds near marshes. But their
song tells us they are there.

Herring Gull

Herring Gull

NO VISIT to the shore would be the same
without the sight of the great white wings of
herring gulls soaring overhead, and the sound of
their mewing cries and loud, cackling laughter.
These big birds gather on sandy beaches and in
harbors everywhere. They follow ships to eat the
food leftovers. Inland, they fly after farmers
plowing their fields to catch the insects that are
stirred up. The young gulls are speckled brown
until they are about four years old.

Common Tern

THE dainty tern is much smaller than the gull, and has a forked tail like a swallow. It skims low over the waves looking for fish, and dives down headfirst when it sees one. It has a nervous, twittering cry.

Common Tern

Chickadees and Titmice

THERE are many kinds of these small, cheerful bundles of feathers. Often they are very friendly, and some will even learn to feed out of your hand. They are always hopping about and, like tiny monkeys, can swing upside down on twigs.

Tufted Titmouse

Black-capped Chickadee

Carolina Chickadee

Chestnut-backed Chickadee

Female

Male

Cardinal

THE most brilliant red bird you'll see will be the male cardinal. He is especially vivid against the snow in winter, for these birds don't travel south in the cold weather. The female cardinal wears quiet, yellowish brown. These birds belong to the same finch family as the canary, which is often kept as a pet songbird. The cardinal, too, has a loud, cheerful song.

Ring-necked Pheasant

THIS handsome bird with the long tail always travels with several wives, not as brightly dressed as he. They walk along the ground, pecking at seeds. The male bird crows like a rooster. At other times pheasants sound like rusty hinges on a gate: *Craik, craik!* Pheasants stay around all winter and you may be lucky enough to see them brightening up a snowy scene, though they can hide very well in brown grasses and weeds.

Ring-necked Pheasant

Male

Female

Bobwhite (Quail)

THE bobwhite looks like a small, fat chicken, bobbing its head as it walks or runs on the ground. When it flies, its wings make a loud, whirring sound as it takes off. Quails lay a lot of eggs at a time (twelve to fourteen) and, after the eggs hatch, you may see the young quails following their parents in single file, picking at seeds in the ground and making little cheeping sounds.

Female

Male

Sparrow Hawk

Falcons and Hawks

FALCONS and hawks, which also hunt small birds and animals, belong to the same family as eagles. They are intelligent birds and have been kept by people who hunt small animals with them.

The OSPREY feeds on fish and is sometimes called a fish hawk. It builds its huge nest in treetops near the shore.

Sharp-shinned Hawk

Osprey

Swans

THE beautiful, dignified swans "tip up" when looking for food. Sometimes they dip their long, graceful necks under water. Swans are very large birds and can be fierce if annoyed.

The babies (or cygnets) are fluffy gray. Sometimes they ride on their mother's back.

Ducks

THERE are many different kinds of ducks on the pond. The one with the handsome green head and white collar is a mallard. The pretty brown and white one is his wife. They are very proud of their downy ducklings. When a duck suddenly "ducks" with his tail in the air, he is not showing off. He is feeding on plants and insects that live under the water.

Red-breasted Merganser

Blue-winged Teal

Mallard

Male   Female

Cormorant

THESE large black birds with the long necks are the world's best fishermen. They dive deep and swim a long way underwater and always seem to come up with a fish. They gather in flocks on every rocky coast, making hardly a sound.

Sandpiper

DOZENS of these little birds gather where the waves break on the shore. As a wave goes back the sandpipers run forward as swiftly as if someone had pulled them on a string. They peck rapidly into the sand to find little crabs and insects—quickly, before the next wave comes in!

Semipalmated Sandpiper

Double-crested Cormorant

41

Latin or Scientific Names of the Birds Shown in This Book

Canada Goose *Branta canadensis* 10–11
English Sparrow *Passer domesticus* 12
Starling *Sturnus vulgaris* 13
Pigeon *Columba livia* 14
Blue Jay *Cyanocitta cristata* 15
Crow *Corvus brachyrhynchos* 16
Magpie *Pica pica* 17
Robin *Turdus migratorius* 18
Wood Thrush *Hylocichla mustelina* 19
Bluebird *Sialia sialis* 19
Bald Eagle *Haliaeëtus leucocephalus* 20
Golden Eagle *Aquila chrysaëtos* 21
Rufous Hummingbird *Selasphorus rufus* 22
Ruby-throated Hummingbird *Archilochus colubris* 23
Barn Owl *Tyto alba* 24
Great Horned Owl *Bubo virginianus* 24
Screech Owl *Otus asio* 24
Downy Woodpecker *Dryobates pubescens* 25
Yellowthroat (top) *Geothlypis trichas* 26
Black and White Warbler *Mniotilta varia* 26
American Redstart *Setophaga ruticilla* 26
Blackburnian (bottom) Warbler *Dendroica fusca* 26
Yellow-rumped or Myrtle (top) Warbler *Dendroica coronata* 27
Yellow Warbler *Dendroica petechia* 27

About the Author

KATHLEEN N. DALY was born in London. She spent her childhood on the island of Mauritius, in the Indian Ocean, and in France and Scotland. Ms. Daly has been a children's book editor in both England and America, and is the author of more than thirty books for children, many of them on the birds, plants, and animals of the world. She now lives in New York City.

About the Artist

FRED BRENNER has been an amateur ornithologist since he was ten years old, and has photographed hundreds of species of birds both professionally and avocationally. Mr. Brenner teaches art at the Parsons School of Design, an affiliate of The New School for Social Research, in New York. He has illustrated a number of children's books, and photographed many of the subjects he illustrated in *A Child's Book of Birds*. Mr. Brenner and his wife, Barbara Brenner, an author of many children's books, live in West Nyack, New York.